How to Use
Your Community
as a Resource

HOW TO

USE YOUR COMMUNITY AS A RESOURCE

Helen H. Carey
Deborah R. Hanka

A Social Studies Skills Book
FRANKLIN WATTS/1983
New York/London/Toronto/Sydney

Photographs by Ginger Giles
Diagrams by Anne Canevari Green

Library of Congress Cataloging in Publication Data
Carey, Helen H.
How to use your community as a resource.

(A Social studies skills book)
Bibliography: p.
Includes index.
Summary: Describes ways of using one's community as a
resource for various kinds of studies; how to make and
use a resource file; how to conduct polls, surveys, and
interviews; and how to research a community's history.
1. Community—Research—United States—Juvenile
literature.   2. Social sciences—Research—United States
—Juvenile literature.   3. Civics—Study and teaching
(Secondary)—United States.   [1. Community] I. Hanka,
Deborah R.   II. Giles, Ginger, ill.   III. Title.
HM131.C256 1983   307'.072   83-12408
ISBN 0-531-04675-3

orig: 7-27-84

J

Contents

To my sisters
Barbara, Marilyn, and Judy

How to Use Your Community as a Resource

Introduction

What are community resources? You are a community resource. And so are your relatives, your teachers, librarians in public and school libraries, government officials, local industrial and business leaders, museum and art gallery guides, and members of historical societies. People are one important resource that every community has. The places and facilities in your community also are community resources. You depend on these resources for education, health care, transportation, safety, entertainment, and recreation.

Have you ever wondered about the people who first settled in your town? Would you like to know more about where they came from and why they settled there? Do you want to learn more about how your town grew and changed over the years? What were the reasons for these changes?

Many community resources can help you find answers to these and other questions. Your research will include more than just taking books out of the library. It will take you outside the classroom walls and into the community itself. In fact, it may take you beyond your hometown to state and national resources.

How to Use Your Community as a Resource will help you discover some of the ways community resources can enrich your life, improve your research skills, and make your social studies lessons come alive. Using the community as a laboratory to conduct study projects about local history, for example, can give you invaluable experience in locating and using information. Your investigation will also help you learn to distinguish between important and unimportant facts, draw conclusions on the basis of sufficient and valid information, and report findings accurately and objectively. You can use these skills while you are in school and after you graduate.

Your research using community resources can result in a fascinating and unique school project. A play about the community's history could be presented to local elementary schools. A movie about the variety of jobs in your city might be shown at both a meeting of local business leaders and a high-school assembly.

Tapping your community's resources—its people, places, and things—can be fun. Charts, graphs, and books are valuable sources of information, but many things can be learned only through speaking and listening. Therefore, to thoroughly investigate a topic related to the local community you will have to conduct interviews and surveys. This book will help you develop the skills you need to get information from talking to people and to record that information.

1

How to Use Community Resources

I f we look carefully at a community, we will find a wealth of fascinating people, places, and things. Each person or place has information to share or a story to tell; it's just a matter of finding them and cultivating the possibilities.

Finding these people and stories is like detective work, and you are the detective. First, you must try to figure out who or what will have the answers. When you find these resources—and often you'll find them in unexpected places—you'll be able to answer your questions and put all the pieces of information together.

As you investigate, you will need to use all the skills described in this book. You will survey various community resources and interview people. You will make firsthand observations. You will take notes and organize information in a resource file. To organize any investigation, whether large or small, you will need to follow these steps:

- Choose the topic.
- Identify research questions and community resources.
- Use community resources in research, through surveys and interviews.

- Refine or redefine the topic.
- Analyze information and draw conclusions.
- Present your findings to others.

CHOOSING THE TOPIC

When choosing a topic to research, you can draw on your hobbies and interests, or ask friends, relatives, or teachers to make suggestions. For example, if you have a keen interest in computers, or other aspects of the new technologies, you may want to do a project studying the changes in family life caused by video games.

Remember that your community may be limited as a resource. If you live in a small town in the Midwest, you probably won't be able to find firsthand information about whaling in New England. A better topic might be the effects of the Great Depression on farming. You'll be able to collect firsthand information from people who lived at that time, newspaper accounts, and public records. Letters, family photograph albums, and diaries also may provide additional information.

However you choose your topic, it should be fairly easy to research, but not one that is flooded with information. The American Revolution may seem to be a good topic at first, but, on second glance, it's just too broad. Libraries have entire shelves of books about the Revolution, and historians dedicate their lives to studying minor events within the Revolutionary War. On the other hand, a project about the lives of lesser-known

Everyone in your community
has information to share
or a story to tell.

Revolutionary War heroes, such as Deborah Sampson and Peter Salem, may be too narrow. Unless they lived in your town or state, finding community resources on single individuals may be too difficult. Better topics are ones that are limited and yet provide enough material. A city's or state's role in the Revolution; the roles of women, blacks, or ethnic groups in the war; or a key battle may be good topics, and the appropriate resources can be found within the community.

Break down your topic into manageable categories to help organize your thoughts and actions. For example, if you are investigating how books are selected for your public or school library, divide your topic into:

- the process of book selection
- limits placed on selections
- individuals responsible for selections
- past methods of book selection

Investigating these one at a time makes information gathering easier. Related issues, such as censorship, freedom of the press, community standards, and book banning may help you think of additional questions.

IDENTIFYING RESEARCH QUESTIONS AND COMMUNITY RESOURCES

You may be familiar with the word "brainstorming." Brainstorming is a group process of coming up with ideas. One person's ideas spark different suggestions from the others. The group takes a topic, then lists all of the other topics it can think of that relate to it. If you need possible research questions for your project, or if you need ideas for resources, brainstorm with your family, friends, or teacher.

*There are all kinds of community resources; your
local television station, for example, may be able
to provide information about disaster preparedness.*

When you brainstorm, list every suggestion made by
others. Later, evaluate the suggestions. You may remove
some and add others. Some will need to be rewritten or
defined. Then organize the suggestions. Soon you will
have a usable list of questions and resources. Below is a
sample topic and lists of related research questions and
community resources. Your research questions and
resources will vary depending on your topic and the community you live in. You may choose to work with only a
few questions at a time, as there may not be time to
research all of them simultaneously.

[7]

Topic: Disaster Preparedness

Possible research questions:

1. What disasters can strike the community?
2. What disasters has this community experienced in the past?
3. What local government agencies and officials are involved in helping people during a disaster?
4. What actions are taken by the National Guard, private organizations, and government?
5. What private or community organizations help?
6. What plans, if any, exist to deal with disasters in the community?
7. Who decides if an area should be evacuated?
8. Where would people go if an evacuation occurred?
9. How would they travel to these places?
10. How can individuals help?
11. What role do community businesses play in solving problems during a disaster?
12. What are the possible effects of a disaster on the community?
13. How are national disaster areas determined?
14. How do state, federal, and local governments help victims?
15. How is order maintained and property protected during a disaster?
16. How might personal freedoms be affected at the time of a disaster?

Possible community resources:

- Local government officials

- Local chamber of commerce
- American Red Cross
- Salvation Army
- Local offices of Emergency Preparedness Services
- National Guard
- Police and fire departments
- Radio and television stations
- Owners of CB radios
- Owners of four-wheel drive vehicles
- Ham radio operators
- National Oceanic and Atmospheric Administration (NOAA)
- Hospitals
- Schools
- Churches
- Public Health Service (Department of Health and Human Services)
- State Departments of Natural/Environmental Resources
- Public utilities (gas, water, electric, sanitation)
- U.S. Army Corps of Engineers
- Businesses
- Center for Disease Control
- National Parks Service
- U.S. Forest Service (Department of Agriculture)
- National Weather Service (U.S. Department of Commerce)
- Department of Transportaton (national, state, and local offices)
- Highway Administration (state)

2

The Community Resource File

Keeping track of all your resources and information can be overwhelming. Organizing this material is easier if you have a system and place to record your research, which we call a *community resource file*. You can set up a file card system or use a loose-leaf notebook, which allows more room for keeping notes. You can even develop your own system. If an entire class is involved in the project, your file could be incorporated with your classmates' files. You may also want to keep your file as a reference for future projects. Your research may spark a personal interest in a new area, and you may want to continue adding to your community resource file over the years.

THE FIRST CONTACT

Before making the initial contact with any of your sources, list the necessary information, including the name of the community resource, address, and telephone number. Leave room for additional information, such as available services and materials, other areas of expertise, business hours, and other people to see. Establish a consistent format and set of abbreviations.

1427 Milestone Road
Metropolis, MD 11235
March 9, 1983

Eve R. Adams
Station HIST
Metropolis, MD 11237

Dear Ms. Adams:

    I am researching the history of my neighborhood
for a school project. Last Saturday I saw you on the
TV show "Voices of Metropolis." You spoke about the
class you teach called Local History: Where to Find
It, What to Ask. Would it be possible to meet you
and discuss my research project? Your assistance
would be most helpful.

    If an interview isn't possible, would you be
willing to answer some questions by mail? I can be
reached by phone at 555-7856 after 4 p.m. I really
appreciate any attention you can give my requests.

                        Sincerely,

                        Paul Carpenter

                        Paul Carpenter

With the names and addresses of your resources recorded on your resource sheets, the next step is to contact them for the first time to arrange an interview. The contact can be made over the telephone or through the mail. The phone is more convenient, although some requests for interviews must be made in writing.

If using the phone for a "cold" call makes you nervous, practice role-playing with a friend. Practicing that first contact call will make the real one easier. (Throughout this book there are exercises to help you use the skills explained here. You may not want to try them all, but some practice is necessary to learn any new skill.)

It is frustrating and time-consuming if a call is shuffled from one office to another or if you are put on hold for a long time. If these things happen, be patient and polite. Speak clearly and slowly so the person can hear your request for an interview, a speaker, printed materials, or tour information. In addition, ask the contact for leads to other community resources.

Having your questions, paper, and pen or pencil ready and your resource card in front of you, quickly write the answers directly on your resource sheet. Or, write them on paper and type them on the sheet or card after the call. It may be easier to read the information later from typed cards.

Some people may provide information or set up a meeting by telephone, and then request that the phone call be followed up by a letter. This gives the person a record of the call and any arrangements that were made. If this happens, be sure to send the letter promptly. Keep a copy of the letter for yourself.

If a resource is found through a newspaper or a television show, your first contact may be through the mail. Letters should be typed. If there is no typewriter available, be sure your handwriting is legible and neat. Make sure your letters are grammatically correct and free from spelling errors. Prepare a rough draft and have someone check the spelling and organization before making the final copy you'll send. A good letter is short and to the point. Don't fill two or three pages.

After the first contact, a completed resource card or sheet should look like this:

Oz Aluminum Company (Resource Name) 555-5555(Phone)
714 Yellow Brick Road
Emerald City, Oz 67106(Address) 9-5 M-F(Hours)

Contact: Tim Mann referred by C. Lyon
Available services: speakers, student experiment programs, plant tours
(Extra Information)
2 wks. notice required for any service

ORGANIZING YOUR FILE

As you begin your research, you may organize your material according to the source of information. For example, your categories may be:

- personal interviews
- taped interviews
- field trips
- surveys
- letters

After the initial contacts have been made, categorize each resource sheet and file it accordingly. Then review the material in your file. If you find out that you need more information, turn to your leads for other resources. As you review your material, similarities and categories may become apparent, and you may want to reorganize your information.

If your topic is "Contributions Made by Immigrants," the areas in which you have found such contributions have been made, such as science, medicine, defense, education, the fine arts, and inventions may become your new categories. A topic about history may have chronological categories. You may decide that the most useful categories for a study of "Changes in Mass Production" are the decades since the 1790s, when Eli Whitney first used interchangeable parts to make guns. Each new development would be filed in the appropriate time period.

You may be able to define your topic in a few basic questions. If you are researching laws dealing with drunk driving, your investigation could be organized around these questions:

- What changes are being made in the laws?
- What groups are bringing these changes about?
- What kind of sentences can drunk drivers expect?

If you are having difficulty in organizing your materials, it may be because your topic is too broad, or you lack some basic information which would help you put the pieces into place. You may need to go back to a source for help in redefining your topic. The organizing process is a good way to find out what questions you still need to ask.

Cross-References

When you organize your files, you'll notice that some information belongs in more than one category. There's no reason to lose track of good information because it is filed under another category. Cross-referencing prevents this from happening. Cross-references act as reminders to use information filed under other categories. Library card catalogs, encyclopedias, and dictionaries use cross-references. Whenever a reference book tells you to "See__" or "See also__" (another topic), that's a cross-reference. You can use cross-referencing in your resource file also.

Listing all cross-references on each and every resource sheet is possible but very time-consuming. A better system would be to make one card for each topic and on it list all cross-references so that they can be seen at a glance. For example, in your research on "U.S. Defense" you found an interesting comment about weapons made by a career soldier named Sergeant Alvin York. It is worth using, but the rest of the interview was about the volunteer army. On a page marked "Weapons," you would write the cross-reference "See Volunteer Army: Sgt. York." When you are working on "Weapons," the sheet will tell you where to find exactly what Sergeant York said. This card can have other cross-references as shown:

Weapons—see:

        Volunteer Army: Sgt. York
        Navy: Cmdr. Sinbad
        Army: West Point

Organizing by Cross-References

One method of organizing research depends on cross-referencing for its structure. File each resource card or sheet alphabetically by name. Once this is done, number the sheets. Instead of changing categories as your research progresses, list all your categories on a master sheet with space below each. Go through the resource sheets or cards one by one and figure out into which categories they fit. Record the card or sheet number under as many categories as are appropriate. Each time a number is recorded, it acts as a cross-reference. A master sheet for a file on "Social Security" can look like this one:

	Social Security	
Speakers 3, 5		History 2, 5
Interviews 2, 6		How System Works 2, 3
Trips 1		Benefits 1, 4
Surveys 1, 4		Problems 1, 4
Printed Material 2, 5		Cost to workers 3, 6

An advantage to this method is that you can see the categorized information at a glance. For example, resource 5 appears under three categories—"Speakers," "Printed Materials," and "History." This means that resource 5 can speak on the history of social security and supply printed materials.

Whatever method you choose to organize your file, make sure it is adaptable to new demands. Spiral notebooks and composition books do not allow for flexibility. Changes in categories shouldn't require redoing each resource sheet in the file. It should be easy to add new information or update your file.

3

In-Depth Research: The Interview

Your community has many interesting stories waiting to be told. Interviews are a way to tap these stories. As you interview, you will meet new people and discover unfamiliar places. Gathering information from many sources for your own original project will help you develop your critical thinking skills. You will have to think of and ask questions, make inferences and comparisons, and draw conclusions.

ARRANGING THE INTERVIEW

As we discussed in chapter 2, many times interviews can be arranged over the telephone, either directly with the individual or through secretaries or assistants. Explain the project so that people will be receptive to the interview. Requests through the mail may be required, which will take longer. If this is the case, use the correct business letter format shown in chapter 2 on page 12. Remember to schedule the interview after school or at a time you can be excused from classes. Make sure the topic, date, time, and place are clearly understood.

PREPARING THE
INTERVIEW QUESTIONS

Your community resource file can help you prepare questions for the interview. Don't do extensive research; do just enough to get a general idea of your interview topics and put them on paper. Brainstorming also will help you come up with questions.

Once your list of questions is complete, evaluate them. Reporters must make sure to ask the who, what, where, when, how, and why of a story. The best interview questions are open-ended, that is, they require more than one- or two-word answers. They elicit explanations, opinions, or anecdotes. Sometimes you can reword a yes-or-no question to make it better. Rearranging the order of the questions also can make a difference. Don't ask personal or embarrassing questions.

A list of questions from a brainstorming session about a lawyer's role in the community might look like this:

1. What do you do on your job?

2. What responsibilities do lawyers have?

3. How much time do you spend preparing a case? Presenting the case in court?

4. Who else works on cases with you? What do they do?

5. Do you know any judges?

6. What kinds of cases have you handled?

7. What was your most difficult case?

Firsthand interviews
will introduce you to
new people and places.

[21]

8. Are you married?

9. Did you pass the bar exam the first time you took it?

10. What makes a case difficult?

11. What training is necessary to become a lawyer?

12. Is it hard to pick jurors?

13. Do juveniles ever come to you for help?

14. Do you like your job?

15. Why are lawyers necessary?

16. Do you have the ambition to be a judge?

It is obvious that improvements must be made in the above list. Both the questions and their order need work. Some questions are not open-ended, others are personal, and, therefore, inappropriate. Some of the questions can be grouped together.

Let's evaluate each question:

1. *What do you do on your job?*
   This question is good, but is repeated by the next question.

2. *What responsibilities do lawyers have?*
   This question is much clearer than question 1; discard question 1.

3. *How much time do you spend preparing a case? Presenting the case in court?*
   This is good, because it leads to a discussion about how work and time are organized.

4. *Who else works on cases with you? What do they do?*
   This question is good, because it leads to a discussion about other jobs in a law office.

5. *Do you know any judges?*
   This is a yes-or-no question (and, of course, lawyers know judges). Change the question to: When law-

yers and judges meet socially, does this affect the outcome of cases? This question will lead to a discussion of impartiality and fair trials.

6. *What kinds of cases have you handled?*
   This is a good question, but it should come earlier, with a follow-up question: Which do you prefer and why?

7. *What was your most difficult case?*
   This is good, but it can be combined with question 10.

8. *Are you married?*
   Throw it out! It is too personal and not appropriate to the topic.

9. *Did you pass the bar exam the first time you took it?*
   Throw this out, too. It is too embarrassing if the answer is "no"; it is not open-ended; and question 11 covers the topic in a better way.

10. *What makes a case difficult?*
    This is good. Combine it with question 7 to become: What case was your most difficult and what made it so?

11. *What is necessary to become a lawyer?*
    This question is good, because it gets into education, bar exams, licensing, attitudes, and ethics much better than question 9; it opens new areas for questions based on the answer.

12. *Is it hard to pick jurors?*
    This is not an open-ended question. It would be better to ask: How do you choose your jurors?

13. *Do juveniles ever come to you for help?*
    This is not open-ended; it is better to ask: When and why would juveniles ask for a lawyer?

14. *Do you like your job?*
    This also is not open-ended; change to: What do you like and dislike about your job?

15. *Why are lawyers necessary?*
    This is OK, but could be reworded: Why are law-yers needed? Use this question to begin the inter-view.

16. *Do you have the ambition to be a judge?*
    This question is probably too personal, unless there are many people in the community already suggest-ing it; and it is not open-ended.

The revised list has better questions, and will result in better answers. The questions are to the point. The answers will provide a very good overview of the lawyer's role:

1. Why are lawyers needed?
2. What responsibilities do lawyers have as part of their job?
3. What kinds of cases have you handled?
4. Which kind do you prefer and why?
5. What case was your most difficult and what made it so?
6. How much time is spent in preparing a case? Pres-enting the case in court?
7. Who else works with you on a case? What do they do?
8. What is necessary to become a lawyer?
9. What do you like and dislike about your job?
10. When lawyers and judges meet socially, does this affect the outcome of cases?
11. How do you choose jurors?
12. When and why would juveniles ask for a lawyer?

The above list is only the basis of your interview. Once there, other questions will come to mind.

PREPARING
FOR THE INTERVIEW

Watching people listen to themselves on tape for the first time is interesting. Many are surprised by the sound of their voices and their speech patterns. They may not realize that they repeat their statements, or interject phrases such as "you know" over and over. What are your speech patterns like? What do you sound like? You can find out and practice interviewing at the same time.

Interview yourself. Make a tape in which you ask and answer your own questions. Then play the tape back. Can you make some adjustments? Most people cough now and then, or their voices crack. They may be nervous. That's natural, but you may have noticed other things that can be improved. Speaking quickly results in slurred words. Remember to slow down. Mumbling or talking to the floor also makes it difficult for others to hear you. Some people drop their voices to practically a whisper at the ends of sentences. Speak clearly and face the person you're speaking to. Actors rehearse their lines many times before performing. Rehearsing the questions will make you feel more comfortable when the actual interview takes place.

Practice with friends or relatives. It's an easy way to become familiar with interviewing and overcome anxiety. Try out your questions. You may not get perfect or sensible answers, but you will find out if you've missed some flaws in your questions. If someone doesn't know what a question means, chances are the person you interview won't either. A question that looks good on paper may not be so good when you actually ask it.

If you want to involve more friends or other classmates, try this exercise. Let people pretend they are celebrities—politicians, actors, even soccer players. Their fictitious identities should be kept secret. The object is to

[25]

ask good interview questions so that the identities can be discovered by those in the "audience." The questions should not require simple yes or no replies; they should be open-ended. By the time the secret identities are discovered, everyone has become a little better at interviewing.

A variation of this exercise would be to reveal the identities from the start, and, through questioning, explore ideas, attitudes, and feelings. This requires more research into the individual personalities, so it is not as easy as the earlier game. It is, however, more like real interview sessions.

Watching good interviews on television, such as those on Sunday morning news shows, also is helpful to would-be interviewers.

Final preparation occurs on the day of the interview. Dress appropriately. If you are going to interview an office worker, blue jeans are not the best choice; they may, however, be appropriate for an interview on a construction site or in a coal mine. Usually, good school clothes are suitable. Whatever you wear, make sure you are neat and clean.

Punctuality is important. Find out beforehand how long it will take you to get to the interview site. Write your questions on paper, and leave room for taking notes. Remember to take this sheet with you along with pens or pencils and some extra paper. If you are going to electronically record the interview, take your recorder and a blank tape. Check to see if your equipment is working before you leave. Batteries should be replaced if you have not used the recorder for a long time. Some recorders require an outlet. If you are touring a plant or factory, you won't be able to use even the longest extension cord. Find out what electrical outlets are available when you call for the interview. Careful preparation of this kind will help to make your interview a success.

BEGINNING
THE INTERVIEW

Once you've arrived, it's a good idea to shake hands with the interviewer. After introducing yourself and explaining your project, you might want to emphasize how you are using the community as a resource. If you feel nervous, don't worry. Your nervousness is natural and will probably disappear as the interview progresses. Sit up straight, facing the person. Then begin to ask questions. Make sure the person has finished answering one question before going on to the next. New questions may arise; others on your list may have to be left out. You may find it necessary to ask the questions in a different order than that in which they appear on your list.

LISTENING SKILLS

It won't matter how good the answers to your questions are if you have poor listening skills. Listening should be active, not passive. That is, the answers should set you thinking about new questions or connections with other ideas. Take notes. (Note taking will be explained in the next section of this chapter.) If something is unclear, ask for clarification. Many names and technical terms may be new to you, so ask for the correct spelling.

To lead into your next question, make an observation about a previous answer. If two of your prepared questions are answered at the same time, quickly add notes under both questions. Try not to repeat the second question. If you do need more information, begin your question with "You mentioned earlier . . . ," and then ask for more information. Approaching questions this way shows that you are thinking and listening.

If the person you're interviewing starts to wander off the topic, ask a question about the topic to bring the interview back on track. Starting a question with "Getting back to . . ." may also help. When a person rambles without letting you say anything, be assertive. Politely interrupt, mentioning the time and the questions still unanswered. You may be able to control the interview by using some of these techniques.

At the end of the interview, ask the resource person if he or she has any other comments. You may get additional information or insights, or references to other community resources.

Be sure to thank the person for their time and assistance before you leave.

TAKING NOTES

Your questions are terrific, your listening skills superb. The interview is interesting and informative. But when you get home to put these ideas in your resource file, you can't read the answers to your questions! What happened? Chances are your note-taking skills are weak.

There are many different ways to take notes. Some people use outlines, others make columns on their papers. Still others use so many abbreviations that their writing looks like a new language. All of these methods are fine if they work for you. Different situations call for different note-taking methods. In an interview, you are somewhat restricted. You have only a certain amount of time. Don't

Taking good notes
while interviewing
is essential.

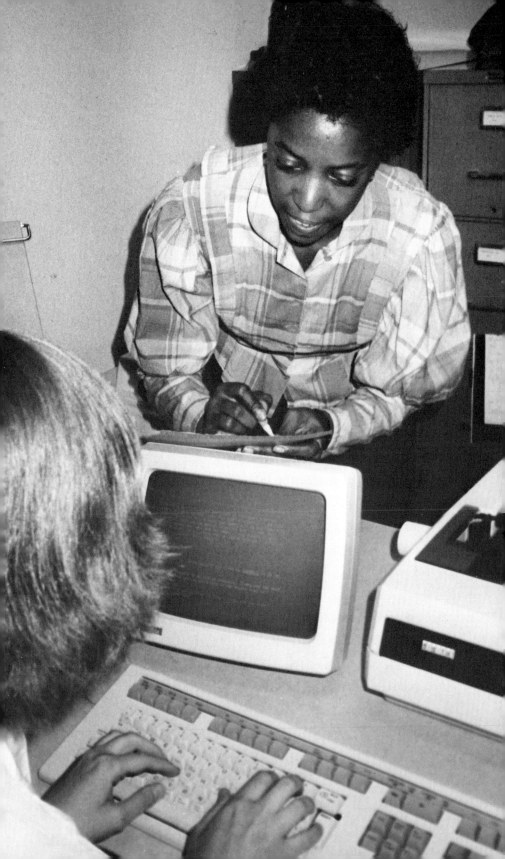

waste it by writing down every word. (You will probably be electronically recording the interview as well.) How can you take notes discreetly, without interfering with the interview process itself, and yet still record all of the important facts?

Using a system of one- or two-word notes, you should be able to record important information. The notes are short and they can later be made into sentences and paragraphs for your resource file. It might be a good idea to figure out beforehand some abbreviations you will need.

The words and phrases you write down should do two things. First, they should represent key ideas. If you choose the wrong words and phrases you may misrepresent the person you are interviewing. Secondly, your notes should mean something to you. They should trigger your memory and help you to recall most of the conversation.

Taking notes isn't easy at first. But practicing will help. You could practice your note taking when you practice your interview questions. Or take notes of a news show or a documentary. Listen to a radio interview and pretend you're the interviewer. Then use your notes to explain the show to another person. This may be harder to do if you wait a day or two before explaining the show, because you will have forgotten what some of the notes mean. This is true also for your actual interviews. For this reason, it's a good idea to review your notes as soon as possible. Transcribe your notes, that is, write them out and place the notes and transcript in your resource file. Make a transcript of the recorded interview as well. Doing this while your memory is fresh will keep your material accurate.

Here is a possible answer from an interview with a political campaign manager. When asked "What problems can occur in a campaign?" this person said:

There are many problems. The biggest, I'd say, is money. Money pays for advertising and publicity for a candidate. Without those, the candidate would have to find other ways to become known. If the opponent has more money, it could mean losing the election. Campaigns are expensive, and people drop out because of a lack of funds. Finding volunteers to work can be a problem, especially if the candidate is unknown. Poor organization also can be a problem. Without good organization, there's wasted effort. That's pretty frustrating: working hard but accomplishing little.

Look at the notes taken from this answer. Notice that the questions were written down before the interview. Space was left for the notes. See if you can figure out the abbreviations.

What problems can occur in a campaign?
1. $ - no money. no advert. & pub.,
   no supp. - lose if oppont. $ - dropouts.
2. Volunteers - lack, esp. if can. unknown
3. organization - if poor, wasted eff. & frust.

One way to check if notes are good is to transcribe them. Written up from these notes, the transcript may look like this:

There are three problems in a campaign. The first and biggest is money. Without money there can be no advertising or publicity, resulting in no support. If an opponent has more money, he or she could win. Others drop out of the race because of a lack of money. The lack of volunteers is also a problem, especially if the candidate is unknown. The third problem, poor organization, can result in wasted effort and frustration.

Even if you are tape-recording the interview, you will need to take notes. If somehow the tape is lost or damaged, you will still have a record of the interview.

INTERVIEW FOLLOW-UP

Finally, write a letter thanking the person you have interviewed. A letter shows that his or her time was really appreciated. Such a letter also speaks well of you. Mention how the project will be presented. You may want to invite the person to share that experience with you. Tell how much the interview helped.

LONG-DISTANCE INTERVIEWS

Personal interviews are fine as long as they can be arranged. But some people may not be available for personal interviews. If you are researching the federal lawmaking process, an interview with your U.S. Senator would be extremely valuable. But suppose the Senate is in session, in Washington, D.C., and you live in California. In this case, a long-distance interview is possible.

Making long-distance telephone calls is a very expensive way of doing long-distance interviews. This just isn't very practical. If you do decide to make long-distance calls, tell the person at the other end that you are calling long distance. Be prepared—have your questions ready and a pencil and paper in hand.

A more practical way to have a long-distance interview is through the mail. Send a letter explaining the project, the time limit involved, and why that person was selected for the project. Send a set of questions with your letter. The questions can be typed or clearly handwritten.

Be sure to leave space for the answers. There is no guarantee that the questions will be answered, but enclosing a stamped, self-addressed envelope will help. Limiting the number of questions also will increase the chances of a return.

There is another way to have a long-distance interview. For this method, both you and your resource need to have a tape recorder. A cassette recorder is best because cassettes are readily available and easy to mail. Record an introduction to yourself on the tape. Explain your topic and that you are using community resources for your research material. Mention that you've included questions that you would like answered. Tell the resource to record the answers on the cassette now being played. Include instructions on how to record the answers. Thank the person for his or her help, ask that the taped answers be returned as soon as possible, and give your return address. A stamped, self-addressed envelope should be sent with the tape. Make sure that the tape is packed safely for mailing.

The biggest advantage to this method is that each person can hear the other's voice, allowing for a more personal interview. This can't be done with letters. As with any of the other kinds of interviews, notes should be transcribed and filed. A letter of thanks should be part of your follow-up.

OTHER SOURCES
FOR IN-DEPTH RESEARCH

People are not the only community resources. Documents, letters, official papers, and personal journals also can be important parts of your research. In an interview, though, you can control what, and how much, information is made available by the questions you ask. When

you are looking at a written text, all the information that the author chose to include is in front of you, much of which may not be relevant to your topic. It is very important for you to know exactly what questions you want answered, so that you can guide your reading. Take notes as you read, and transcribe and file them as soon as possible.

You can learn from people, texts, and objects, and you can learn from places. Visiting the places that are community resources is fun, and your topic will come to life. Use your observation skills. Traveling across your state can be a lesson in geography. Visiting an archaeological site can give you a feeling for how earlier peoples lived. Do some basic research on how the place you are to visit is related to your topic. Develop a set of questions that can be answered through your observations or by others at the location.

As you tour a site, take notes on what you see, hear, feel, and taste. Your impressions are what make these trips important. Some of your questions will be answered and others will come to mind. Visiting a Civil War home may answer your questions about how people lived then by giving you a chance to see the tools, furniture, and utensils in the home. If the guides are dressed in period costumes, you will realize how hot the clothes must have been for the wearer. You also will realize that washing and ironing clothes must have been hard work. New questions about the roles of men and women may suggest themselves to you.

A picture of an assembly line or an office filled with computers gives no clue as to how noisy these places are.

Quickly sketch a building
or historic site to
record visual impressions.

When you visit one of these sites, you might want to ask about how the workers' hearing is affected.

Quick sketches or even photographs, if allowed, are excellent ways to record visual impressions. Be sure to ask permission before photographing a site. If there is no time for photos or drawings on the tour, make the sketches after the trip. At some sites printed material is available. File your transcribed notes, sketches, printed material, and tour information for future use. If the tour was arranged especially for you, send a thank-you letter.

If you are doing a project on community history, you can explore old buildings such as train stations, warehouses, college campuses, or churches. Request permission so that you don't trespass. If your project concerns the architecture of Victorian houses or Art Deco movie theaters, for example, take a sketchbook with you to draw details.

Suppose that your topic is colonial life, and to research this topic you visit a restored home. The objects in the house and the house itself vividly reveal colonial lifestyles. Right there you decide that your final project should be taking your classmates on a tour of this home. As you walk from room to room, you make specific observations about everything. Later, you transcribe your notes and use them to design questions that will help guide your classmates' observations when they visit the same place.

You might ask how tall the people were who lived there. Because of the low doorways and small beds, you know that they were short. Will others find more evi-

Photograph interesting places
and objects, but be sure to
get permission first.

[36]

dence to support that conclusion? You might write questions about food and its flavor. Will others notice what spices were in the kitchen? Fireplaces, candlesticks, and candle molds could lead to questions about fuel and energy. The presence of a loom and a leather vest might give rise to questions about clothing and tools. Once back at school, you can lead a discussion on everyone's observations.

The best questions are those which depend on observation for the answers. Remember to include special considerations for students who are handicapped.

4

Polls and Surveys

A *survey* consists of taking information from a small sample of people in order to learn something about a whole population. Surveys are often called *polls*. Learning how to construct and analyze surveys are important social studies skills.

A survey is useful when you:

- want to find out how a particular group of people feels about an issue
- need information that can't be found in any other place
- need to collect information quickly and efficiently

Sampling can be compared to putting a thousand different-colored marbles in a box, then picking out twenty of the marbles at random, not looking at the colors. The percentage of marbles of each color in the sample should come fairly close to the percentage of those of each color for the total number of marbles in the box.

How is sampling actually done? Dr. George Gallup of the Gallup Organization used a 1,500-person sample to estimate the views of 225 million people. Imagine 225 million marbles in an enormous box. These marbles represent the people of the United States. Let us suppose that the various colors of the marbles represent the different opinions of the total population. Fifteen hundred marbles chosen at random should represent the proportion of these different opinions in relation to the total population. Just as you don't need to count all the marbles of every color in order to find out how many of each there are, a Gallup poll doesn't survey the entire United States population. Gallup's 1,500-person sample can give a reliable estimate.

Many of the polls and surveys you make will use the principle of sampling. If you choose your sample carefully, you will be able to project the larger population's opinion from your sample. Of course, the size of your population and sample will be much smaller than those of a Gallup poll. You will base the size of your sample group on an estimate of the size of the total population you will be surveying, such as your community, neighborhood, school, or class.

DESIGNING A SURVEY

Maybe you've heard about a proposal for a rating system similar to that for the movies to help parents guide their children's television viewing. A survey can help you determine whether people feel there is a need for a rating system for TV shows. It might also show how people feel about rating systems in general.

Once you have decided to conduct a survey, you must take the following steps:

1. Define the issue.
2. Define the sample, that is, the groups who should be included in the survey.
3. Write the questions you will be asking.

4. Conduct the survey.

5. Analyze and present the results.

STEP 1. *Defining the Issue.* Carefully state on paper the issue or trend you want to find out about. For example, are you interested in finding out why people might want a TV-rating system? Do you want to know how many and what sort of people want ratings? Do you want to know if the rating system should be for all shows or only prime-time shows? Do you want to find out about opinions on cable-TV shows as well as those of the major networks?

If you don't carefully define the issue, your survey won't reveal anything significant.

STEP 2. *Defining the Group.* Are you interested in all viewers? Or will you survey teenagers, parents and grandparents, viewers in your neighborhood, or students in your class? You must draw limits somewhere or you may end up asking too many people, or asking inappropriate people, such as those who don't watch TV.

Your sample can be larger if you use several interviewers. One interviewer could survey some specific group or just part of the overall sample.

STEP 3. *Writing the Questions.* This is probably the most difficult task. Your questions require careful wording. Simple, easy-to-understand questions are best. Long, complicated questions tend to confuse people. If they don't have a clear idea of what you mean, you will not get answers you can rely on.

On the television-rating questionnaire, one of your first questions should make clear what you mean by a rating system. People who aren't sure just what you mean are likely to either skip the question, or answer part of it, or guess at the meaning. Thus, it's entirely possible for many answers to be incomplete or impossible to count as fair. As a result, your survey will be less reliable. Look at the same question stated two ways:

Question:	Should there be a rating system for TV shows? Tell why.
Improved:	Should TV use a rating system that advises viewers when a show has a lot of violence, sex, and swear words? Tell why.

Both questions use simple, clear language, a must for all questionnaires. The second question offers a better explanation of what is meant by a rating system, but it still may not be entirely clear to all people. They probably will need more information on how a rating system for TV shows will work before they can answer how they feel about it. Comparing the television-rating system to that used for the movies might make it clearer.

The weakest part of both questions is asking people to tell why they think the way they do. Will many people want to take the time to discuss this in detail or write a lengthy explanation? You can make it easier for people to respond to a survey if you eliminate as many questions requiring wordy answers as possible. This will also make the questionnaire easier for you to evaluate. Ask respondents to check or circle their opinions.

You could ask the question this way:

Should TV use a rating system similar to that for the movies to advise viewers that a show has a lot of violence, sex, and swear words in it? Circle the category of each type of show that you feel should be rated:

Movies on TV
Saturday cartoons and children's shows
Daytime soaps
Prime-time shows
Family-hour shows
All TV shows, except news
All TV shows, including news
No programs should be rated

Each person given a questionnaire must be asked exactly the same questions. You can get very different answers by changing the wording of a question even slightly. If you are surveying in person, one way to make sure the questions are always the same is to read them from a prepared sheet.

It's always a good idea to pretest your survey questions to find out if they "work." It is impossible to anticipate all the possible misunderstandings that might arise from the questions. If you pretest the questions by asking a few people to fill out the questionnaire, you will be able to reword questions that are not clear enough or that are an invasion of privacy, such as "How much do you weigh?" or "How much money do you make?"

Everyone who responds to your survey should be kept anonymous. People feel freer to answer questions, particularly about sensitive issues, when they know their opinions will be kept secret. Identifying respondents by number instead of name is one way you can preserve anonymity and still keep track of the number of questionnaires that are filled out. If you are conducting a survey by personal interview, try to make doubly sure to keep the respondent's identity secret.

QUESTIONNAIRE

Interview No.

HOW DO PEOPLE FEEL ABOUT A TV-RATING SYSTEM?

Circle the appropriate category

Age Group
14–16 17–21   Male   No. of   No. of
22–29 30–49   Female   Children   Grandchildren
   50–Over

Survey Method	Advantages	Disadvantages
Personal interviews	Good for collecting a great deal of information.	Time-consuming.
Telephone interviewing	Quick method for getting information.	Difficult to "screen" for particular respondents, such as girls of a particular age group. People may not be available when you call.
Mail surveys	Good to use with members of particular groups, such as 4-H Clubs or Scouts.	Names and addresses are hard to get. The number of responses is often low. The cost of postage must be considered.

STEP 4. *Conducting the Survey.* Once the questions are written and pretested, it is time to conduct the survey. You can conduct surveys in several ways: by mail, telephone, and personal interview. Each type of survey method has several advantages, but also some disadvantages, as the chart above illustrates.

To get a quick sample of opinions about a subject, interview people on a busy street corner.

Also, the sort of people you need to interview for your survey and the number of people you plan to interview will help you to decide which survey method is best for you. For example, if you wanted to know the opinion of working people in general on a certain subject, you could conduct personal interviews at lunchtime on a downtown corner, or at a busy commuter stop in the morning or evening. If you wanted to survey a smaller, more particular group, you might use a telephone interview, or a mailed questionnaire if you had more time.

Hints for a Good Survey

Careful preparation is essential for good surveys. There are several things that can get your survey into trouble:

- not having enough questionnaires and other materials on hand
- failing to follow up on telephone calls, letters, and postcards
- not checking the progress of the survey on a regular basis
- poorly prepared interviewers

Gather all necessary materials for the survey ahead of time. Prepare a folder for each interviewer, with several copies of the questionnaire, a letter of introduction from your teacher or leader, a statement about the purpose of the poll and the way it is to be used, and anything else to be shown, or read over the phone, to the person who is being interviewed.

Before you begin a telephone survey, send letters explaining the purpose of the survey and the fact that an interviewer will be calling soon. The letter should state that the name of the person being interviewed will be

kept private and that responding to the survey is voluntary. Explain how the answers are to be used. Remember to consider the costs of stamps whenever you decide to contact your sample by mail.

Include a stamped postcard with your letter to be filled out and returned to you.

16

Interview Number

☐ I am willing to take part in your survey.

☐ I am not willing at this time to take part in the survey.

The best time to call is

(Please circle)

Weekday morning	Weekday afternoon	Weekday evening	Saturday only
M T W Th F	M T W Th F	M T W Th F	

Other
_____

If the respondents circle particular days of the week they wish to be called, by all means make the call then. You may lose the important groups you want represented in your survey if you fail to do this.

It is also very important to check on the progress of the survey almost daily. Checking can tell you whether or not

- people understand the questions or are answering each question
- people are returning their questionnaires (if you are using a mail survey)
- interviewers are getting the job done on time (if you are using personal interviews)
- people in selected groups are being contacted and interviewed
- groups are being represented fairly and that substitute interviews are not carelessly made

Preparing Interviewers. You can train yourself and others ahead of time to make sure your survey is conducted properly. Training means practicing such points as:

- how to approach the people you want to interview
- how to conduct the interview in a professional manner
- how to avoid influencing the people being surveyed

One good way to begin the training is to hold practice interviews with your classmates. Form pairs and take turns acting out the part of the interviewer and the part of the person being interviewed. Practice conducting an interview in person and by telephone.

Practice a variety of situations that you are likely to encounter. Some examples of difficult interviewees are:

Practice conducting an interview over the phone before you begin a telephone survey.

- people who are in a hurry and don't want to be bothered
- people who are suspicious about how the survey results will be used
- people who resent calls at home because they feel their privacy is being invaded
- people who are not very familiar with the English language
- people who want to talk endlessly about the survey questions

You and your classmates should decide what adjustments should be made by the interviewer in these situations.

Hold a discussion after each practice session. Talk about approaches that put people at ease and those that distract or annoy them. All of the following approaches work most of the time:

FOR PERSONAL
INTERVIEWS

- shaking hands when you introduce yourself
- being cheerful and greeting people with a smile
- being as enthusiastic about the survey as you can
- dressing to create the best possible impression

FOR TELEPHONE
INTERVIEWS

- identifying yourself first when you call someone on the phone
- using a pleasant tone and speaking clearly and naturally

List the characteristics that yield successful interviews, and contrast these with characteristics that make for poor ones. Discuss ways you can make poor interviews into successful ones.

Finally discuss some appropriate ways to bring the interview to a close.

A survey must remain objective and impersonal if the results are to be reliable. Discuss with your classmates some of the ways interviewers can reveal bias toward some answers through personal mannerisms or tone of voice. Suggest methods for changing these behaviors during the interviews. It would be helpful to list your most obvious mannerisms. Then, conduct a mini-poll (five to ten people) to find out which of these mannerisms (smiling, frowning, nodding your head, raising your eyebrows) people think could influence their responses to questions.

STEP 5. *Analyzing and Presenting Results.* The final tasks in conducting a survey are to collect all the answers and analyze and present them. First tabulate all the answers you received. Then determine the results by averaging answers or by figuring percentages. For example, you may want to know the average age of those polled in your survey. Add together the ages of each person, then divide that figure by the number of people questioned. This number represents the average age in your sample, although no one in the sample may be exactly this age.

Averaging may not work well for all surveys. Suppose you surveyed your community to find out how many eighteen-year-olds who are eligible to vote have actually registered. Your tabulated results may look like this:

registered voters: ⅏ ///
nonregistered voters: ⅏ ⅏ //

To present your findings, you must determine percentages. Begin by totaling the number of responses for each

[51]

answer. Divide the number of responses for one answer by the total number surveyed. In this case, to find the percentage of those who registered, divide eight by twenty. (8 ÷ 20 = .40) This means that 40 percent of those surveyed have registered. What percent have not registered? See the table below to check your answer.

	Total Answers	Percentage
yes	8	40%
no	12	60%
Total	20	100%

The survey determines what method—averaging or percentages—will be most helpful in analyzing results.

Once you have completed averaging, make some general conclusions based on your findings. For example, this survey shows that eighteen-year-olds are not interested enough in the voting to register. This conclusion gives rise to certain questions you might look into:

- Why aren't eighteen-year-olds more interested in voting?
- Who registers more frequently—males or females?
- How often do registered eighteen-year-olds vote?

You can present your survey results and conclusions in a number of ways. Tables are a good method but graphs are more striking visually. Differences and similarities can be seen easily in a bar or circle graph or even in a cartoon. Maps, illustrations, and even objects like play money can be used in your presentation.

18-YEAR-OLDS REGISTERED

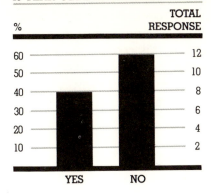

18-YEAR-OLDS REGISTERED

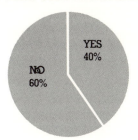

20 SURVEYED

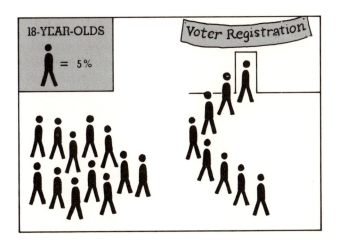

Remember that your survey is accurate for the group you questioned at the time you made the survey. Tomorrow another group or even the same group may have entirely different opinions. For this reason, professional pollsters always indicate when the poll was taken. Going back to the same selected groups several months later is useful when you want to determine changes in opinion over time.

5

Researching
Your Community's
History

One day in social studies, the teacher, after dividing the class into groups of six, announced two challenges. One was to research a topic about the community and present the findings. The second was to do that research by using the community, not just books. The class had spent time discussing the different ways researchers find information, and had even practiced some of them. Every person in each group was to be assigned a research task. Later, each group would coordinate its results and present its conclusions in a special project.

After a brainstorming session, the class compiled this list of topics:

- history
- jobs
- manufacturing and industry
- transportation
- communication
- government
- public safety (fire, police)
- health care

- recreation
- minorities
- religion
- education

Each group in the class was then assigned a topic from among those on the list. The groups brainstormed again, and came up with questions about their topics and places and people that might provide the answers. The history group made the following list:

Questions:
- Who first settled in our community?
- How did they live?
- What major events and changes have taken place in the community since its beginnings?

Resources:
- historical societies
- museums
- newspapers
- letters and other personal papers
- legal records and documents
- longtime residents
- church records
- cemeteries
- family Bibles, photograph albums
- local government offices

The group decided to use a survey to discover the roots of the community's residents, their average age, and the number of years they had lived in the community. Chris and Lee agreed to get started on the survey right away. They wanted to be sure that the answers would be returned in time. Pat volunteered to visit historical homes and record observations made at each place. Dana, Robin, and Jan wanted to interview older residents. Kerry volunteered to keep the community resource file and to make sure everyone worked on schedule. This was important because they had a time limit of three weeks.

The resource file was set up with the three categories corresponding to the research questions, that is, "People," "Lifestyles," and "Changes." The resource cards looked like this:

```
┌─────────────────────────────────────────────────────────────┐
│                                                              │
│   Name                          Address                      │
│                                                              │
│   Position                                                   │
│                                                              │
│   Company/Organization          Phone                        │
│                                                              │
│   ---------------------------------------------------------- │
│                                                              │
│   PEOPLE          LIFESTYLES          CHANGES                │
│                                                              │
│                                                              │
│                                                              │
│                                                              │
└─────────────────────────────────────────────────────────────┘
```

Each group member recorded information on the card after the interview, survey, or visit was completed. Kerry kept all of the cards together in a safe place.

Chris and Lee chose to use a sample of twenty people, randomly selected from the telephone directory. The group was divided equally between women and men to represent the population of the community. Calls were made ahead of time to explain the project and to make sure the person was willing to participate. If so, the survey was mailed to them with a stamped, self-addressed envelope. When the surveys were returned, the results were analyzed, conclusions were drawn, and the information was recorded on the resource card under "People."

Here is their questionnaire:

COMMUNITY HISTORY

How many years have you lived in our community? _____

How many years has your family lived here? _____

What are your national origins? _____

Please return this survey within one week.

THANK YOU FOR YOUR HELP

The three people interviewing longtime residents found five people who agreed to be interviewed. Two of these turned out to be excellent sources of information, and were interviewed in depth.

During her interview, Mrs. Fisher showed Dana the diary her great-great grandmother kept during her first years in America. Because she had settled in the community one year after her arrival, the diary was an excellent account of the community's earliest history. Mr. Chester, who came from a long line of railroaders, had a collection of train memorabilia that filled his entire basement. Maps, pictures, ticket stubs, souvenirs such as menus from the dining cars, train schedules, lists of ticket prices, and posters all helped to tell how important railroads were to the community.

The information from each interview was recorded in the proper category on the resource cards. Once all the interviews were completed, Dana, Robin, and Jan discussed their findings and decided what information was appropriate to their community history project. They also talked about what objects would be helpful in the group's final presentation.

Pat found a list of old homes in the public library. Each home tour helped to put together a record of the lifestyles of the community. Pat's observations also were recorded on the resource cards.

After the research was completed, the group met to share ideas and information. The notes on the resource cards helped refresh the memories of the group members. They discussed all of the answers they had found to their three research questions. They discovered that no single resource provided them with a complete picture of the community's history, but that the written documents, oral information, and actual observations did. The group decided that a panel discussion would be a good way to present its research. On the scheduled day, each person explained his or her findings and how they were obtained.

PRESENTING THE PROJECT

A panel discussion is just one of the many ways to present a community resource project. The possibilities are nearly endless. As you read through the following list, think of other ways you could present what you know about your community's history.

- Paint a mural.
- Make stand-up pictures in a box. Include memorabilia in the display.
- Put on a play or compose a song.
- Invite members of the community to give a talk.

*Above: A panel discussion is one
of many ways to present a school
project using community resources.
Opposite: You can make a montage
of photographs, documents,
and other materials.*

- Draw maps to show the way in which your city grew.
- Make a scrapbook of written materials, souvenirs, and samples from collections.
- Make a montage of photographs, items from collections, and written accounts.
- Prepare a display board of facts about your community. Tell visitors what they will find interesting in each.
- Arrange a bulletin board display about your research.
- Design a game using the information from your work for children or adults to play. The game board might be a map of your community.
- Write a book for children. After the project ends, give the book to your local library for others to use.
- Make and show a film documentary about your community.

A REVIEW OF
COMMUNITY HISTORY RESOURCES

Let us now review the various community resources and how they can provide information about the community's history:

People. It is possible to find people who have lived in your community for forty or fifty years. Their personal recollections can help you verify and enhance what you have read. Sources that can help you locate these people include: the Chamber of Commerce, mayor's office, local government officials' offices, and special historical societies such as the Daughters of the American Revolution (DAR).

Local libraries. Many libraries keep historical collections of the city or community. You can find many books, photographs, old diaries, early maps, local histories, and records of prominent citizens or their published works. Librarians are available for advice, and they will often tell you of other sources for the information you are seeking if they do not have it in their library.

Newspapers. Most communities have had several newspapers over the past centuries. Check first with those newspapers currently being published. They will have back issues on file or important clippings from the old papers. If your newspaper has been published continuously over the years, its files will provide a rich source of information.

Letters and Written Records. Besides the local library, historical association, and newspapers, another source of information are letters from former residents that people in your community may have. Finding these letters may take some perseverance, but your efforts will be worth it. Don't expect to be able to bring these letters and written accounts into class, however. You may, however, be permitted to take notes or copy the parts that you need. Various public offices can also provide material. Census reports, records of land sales, zoning plans, birth and death records, licenses, immigration records, and other official documents are important resources. You may be able to copy or have copies sent to you. If not, take notes on the written records you use.

Maps. Maps of your community can show you many things about the development of your area. Your local planning agency has a historical and archaeological division which may publish material about changes in the community. For example, it may have prepared comparisons between old maps and current street maps, which reveal where changes have taken place. Check also for maps at your community's information center, Chamber of Commerce, the historical society, and the National Parks Service and State Park Service. Maps are often available at gas stations. Community street maps can be found in local stores.

Artifacts. What are artifacts? Old quilts, sewing samplers, paintings, arrowheads, toys, cooking utensils—all of these are artifacts. Besides museums and historical societies, perhaps the best places in the community to look for artifacts are old homes, antique shops, old buildings and churches, and in the archaeology department of a local university. Many antique dealers are experts in the history of furniture, hand and machine tools, and other items. They can refer you to other people or places to visit. You can locate the names of dealers at antique auctions, flea markets, and in telephone directories under "Antiques" or "Collectibles."

Memorabilia and Collectibles. These are objects people keep and collect because they have sentimental, aesthetic, or monetary value, or contain important information. They can be used as sources to help you put together a history of your community.

Look in your own house. Attics and basements may contain valuable items. Old school pictures, for example, can reveal many things besides the changing styles of clothing. You can note the number of students in a class-

Your local newspaper may have files or old clippings which can be a rich source of information.

[64]

NEW LINE BETWEEN
ALBANY & NEWBURG

On and after MONDAY, October 15th,

ST. NICHOLAS

CAPTAIN WILSON,

MONDAYS, WEDNESDAYS & FRIDAYS

AT SEVEN O'CLOCK A.M.

NEW ARRANGEMENT!
Daily Accommodation Line of Stages from
North Castle
TO
PORT CHESTER.

IN CONNECTION WITH THE
New-York and New Haven R. R.

LEAVE PORT CHESTER
LEAVE NORTH CASTLE

HIRAM PURDY, Proprietor.

room, the kinds of desks and school supplies, the size and type of school building, and, perhaps, the playground equipment that was used. Later you can compare these visual impressions with written material and oral histories.

You can find the names of collectors in the Yellow Pages under "Coins" or "Coin Galleries," "Cards," "Souvenirs," and "Keepsakes," to mention a few. Flea markets issue catalogs which list collectors. Many collectors publish information about their collections, which can range from comic books to campaign buttons to movie posters. Look in your local newspapers or in specialized publications for names of collectors.

Buildings and Historic Sites. Buildings, monuments, statues, and old cemeteries are valuable resources. Historic markers on buildings and by the roadside can provide much fascinating information. Field trips and walking tours are the best ways to collect information from these sources. Many walking tours are led by trained people. Sometimes there is a small fee. Try the historical society or local museum for tours. Your Chamber of Commerce has a list of old buildings and places to see.

Another place to look for information is your state's historical trust. It has a wide selection of books on the historic preservation of old buildings. Architects and architecture students at local universities can help you understand the structural and stylistic changes that have been made during your community's growth and development.

Museums and historical societies are the places to find historical objects and artifacts.

Archaeological Digs. It is often possible to find archaeological digs in or near your community. Check first with your local university's archaeology department. Then see what information the museum has on tribes of native Americans or early settlers in the community region.

CONCLUSION

Any community can be a resource for those who know how to use it. By following the suggestions and guidelines given in this book, you can carry out your own investigations using community resources.

As you complete your research, you'll notice that you have gained new skills and improved your old ones. Setting up and following a schedule are important skills. Knowing the time limit on your project, you can determine how much time is to be spent on each stage of the investigation.

Conducting a survey and an interview also are important skills which you will sharpen. Doing surveys and interviews will help improve your social skills as well. You will learn how to develop good questions to guide your research. Another ability that you will improve is active listening to find the meaning of a person's words, and to find the ideas and feelings behind those words. Note taking is another skill you will develop. In order to write accurate notes of an interview you must think clearly and quickly. Organizing information is another important skill that you will sharpen with the help of your community resource file.

Working with other people on your research helps you learn how to cooperate and make compromises. Without these skills, little can be accomplished in any setting where people work together.

Whenever you choose your topic, select a method of investigation, assign tasks to group members, or choose questions to ask, you are demonstrating another skill, that of decision making. Learning how to make careful decisions about your time and research efforts prepares you for making better decisions about your time and effort in other areas.

Your understanding of the community also will change. You will discover that both your community and its resources are unique. Perhaps you'll discover that your entire town was moved at one time to mine the iron ore that had been under it, or that there were five different tribes of native Americans who hunted in your area before settlers arrived.

Finally, a change can occur in your personal involvement in the community. Through community resources, you are more aware of your community, its potential, and its problems. This awareness can lead you to become active in developing this potential and solving these problems. A project on disaster preparedness can reveal deficiencies in plans that must be corrected to prevent lives being lost in a flood. After investigating the growth of your neighborhood, you might testify at a zoning hearing, or help turn a vacant lot into a playground. You can become a member of a local historical society after tracing your community's history, and share your knowledge with other members. A project on the election process can lead to working in a voter registration booth.

Whatever you research, you are an important and active part of your community. You influence every part of the community you contact. You can share your discoveries with others. By doing this, you are making a unique contribution to your community's living history.

Research Topics and Community Resources

KNOWING YOUR NEIGHBORHOOD

Possible Questions to Research:

What are the location and boundaries of your neighborhood?

What is its history?

Where did the first settlers come from?

Are there any original residents?

Why do people choose to live here?

What types of housing, industry, businesses, schools, government services, recreation, medical care, and police and fire protection exist in your neighborhood?

What racial or ethnic groups live in the neighborhood?

What religions are represented?

Do people hold different political beliefs and ideas?

Who are the leaders of the neighborhood?

Who are the well-known people living here?

What activities are there for preschool children, grade school children, teenagers, adults, and senior citizens?

What kinds of clubs, groups, and associations are in your
neighborhood?
What problems exist in your neighborhood?

Possible Community Resources:

Your neighbors
You and your family
Local newspaper office
Zoning commission
Parks and planning
department
Senior citizens association
Nursing home
Churches, synagogues
Library
Historical society
Civic associations
Chamber of Commerce

Business clubs
Shopkeepers and
storeowners
Real estate salesworkers
Lawyers
Local officials
Police officers
Teachers
School administrators
League of Women Voters
U.S. Census Bureau
Local women's and
men's clubs

MANUFACTURING AND INDUSTRY

Possible Questions to Research:

What are your community's most important industries?

What goods and services do these industries provide?

Where is most of the industry located?

Are there any manufacturing plants in your community?

Where are the plants located? Why?

What natural resources are important to these industries?

Where do these resources come from?

How are the raw materials and manufactured goods moved to and from these plants?

How many workers do these industries employ?

What kinds of work do they do?

How are the workers in these industries both producers and consumers in the community?

Who are the consumers of the goods and services provided by these industries?

What problems does each industry face?

How are they solving these problems?

What safety standards and environmental laws apply to these industries?

Who enforces these regulations?

Do the industries pay taxes? If so, how much do they pay?

What labor organizations are involved in local industries?

How does industry help the community?

Are there any negative effects on the community?

How have computers changed the way products are made?

What changes might occur in the next decade—prices, organization, automation, demand for labor?

Possible Community Resources:

Industry employees

Factory or industry public information officer

Stockholders and management of an industry

Mayor or county-executive office

County or city planning office

Zoning commission

Newspaper offices

Library

Phone book

City or county public records office

State and federal departments of labor and commerce
Road, elevation, political, physical, and/or land use
   maps
Census Bureau
Utility companies
Chamber of Commerce
Railroad office
Trucking companies
Union offices
Occupational Safety and Health Administration
Local tax collector's office

COMMUNICATIONS

Possible Questions to Research:

What methods of communication are found in the community?

What methods existed when the community was first established?

Why is communication important?

How is freedom of expression guaranteed in the community?

Why are the First Amendment freedoms so important to communication in a free society?

What restrictions are there on freedom of speech and on freedom of the press?

What role does the government play in communications?

How do other countries and governments handle communication?

What role does mass media play in communications?

What media are protected under freedom of the press besides printed matter?

How are decisions made for programming, news coverage, and editing materials on TV and radio stations?

What is the role of censorship?

How are censorship and propaganda related?

How are individuals affected by the media?

How does the post office handle the mail?

What alternatives are there to the U.S. Postal Service?

What methods of communication are available for the visually-, speech-, and hearing-impaired person?

How has the telephone expanded personal, business, and scientific communications?

How has technology changed communication? What role do satellites play?

What might communications be like in the future?

What careers are open in communications?

Possible Community Resources:

Federal Communications Commission
Local newspaper offices
Commercial TV and radio stations
Public Broadcasting System
Campus newspapers and broadcasting studios
Post office
The U.S. Constitution
Law offices
Government attorneys
Law schools
Bookstores and newsstands
National Coalition on Television Violence
School boards
Book committees for schools and public libraries
Federal and state departments of education
Computer industries

Satellite industries
Phone companies
State, local, and private agencies for the handicapped
Counseling centers
National Aeronautics and Space Administration
   (NASA)
Historical societies
Action for Children's Television
Parent-Teacher Association
Advertising agency

JOBS AND CAREERS

Possible Questions to Research:

What jobs do people have in your community?
What factors make a job or career a good choice for a
   person?
How do you find out about job requirements?
How do you find out about job openings?
How do you read a want ad?
How do employment agencies operate?
How do you fill out applications?
How do you write a résumé?
What careers in your community require:
   no high school diploma?
   a high school diploma?
   a college degree?
   an advanced degree?
   specialized training?
What training and educational opportunities can be
   found in your community?
What do employers look for in potential workers?
How do you prepare for an interview?
Who could give you references?

Are some references better to use than others?

What do you need to know about yourself when you look for a job?

What are some questions that you should ask at an interview?

What is an Equal Opportunity Employer?

What nontraditional areas of work are men and women in your community now entering?

Possible Community Resources:

Private employment agencies

State and local employment agencies

Personnel managers in businesses, stores, or factories

High school business teachers

Job counseling centers and business schools

Libraries

Union offices

Military recruiting offices

Vocational and technical schools

Colleges and universities

Guidance counselors

Parents, relatives, neighbors

Civil Service Commission

Chamber of Commerce

Local employers and employees of various businesses in your community

ELECTING OUR LEADERS

Possible Questions to Research:

Which public offices are elected positions, and which are appointed?

What are the qualifications for a specific office?
How does a person declare his/her candidacy?
What is a political convention?
What is the difference between open and closed primaries?
How are convention delegates chosen?
Who sets up election rules and holds elections?
What rules and procedures must be followed in the balloting?
Where do people vote?
How are districts and precincts determined?
How do people learn about candidates?
How are election campaigns funded?
What rules apply to TV and radio air time in elections?
How do citizens register to vote?
What requirements must be met to vote?
How can a person lose his or her voting rights?
How are ballots marked? How are they counted?
How are absentee ballots used?
What percentage of eligible voters are registered? What percentage of these actually vote?
What role do endorsements of candidates by unions, professional organizations, or business leaders play?
What problems are there with our election system?
What improvements could be made in your community?

Possible Community Resources:

Democratic and Republican state and local committees
Independent-party headquarters
Local Board of Election supervisors
Elected officials in municipal, county, state, and national government
League of Women Voters

Libraries
TV and radio stations
Newspaper and magazine offices
Campaign headquarters for candidates
Registered voters
Pollsters or survey takers
Polling places
Political action committees for unions, professional associations, special-interest groups, and businesses
Election judges

For Further Reading

Boyd, Jessie, et. al. *Books, Libraries, and You*. New York: Charles Scribner's Sons, 1965.

Brady, John. *The Craft of Interviewing*. New York: Vintage Books, 1976.

Brandt, Sue R. *How to Write a Report*. New York: Franklin Watts, 1980.

Edison, Michael and Susan Heiman. *Public Opinion Polls*. New York: Franklin Watts, 1972.

Ghory, Ward. *The Study of Neighborhoods: High School Students Explore Their Community*. Chicago: Center for New Schools, 1975.
(Essay based on a high school project in Cincinnati, Ohio, to explore neighborhoods in the city by taking tours led by neighborhood residents, interviewing community spokespeople about political and social issues, and by researching historical statistical data.)

Gilfond, Henry. *How to Give a Speech*. New York: Franklin Watts, 1980.

Gorden, Charlotte. *How to Find What You Want in the Library*. Woodbury, NY: Barron's Educational Series, 1978.

Howard, Vernon. *Talking to an Audience*. New York: Sterling Publishing, 1967.

James, Elizabeth and Carol Barkin. *How to Write a Term Paper*. New York: Shepard Books, 1980.

_____. *Using Community Resources*. Chicago: Follett Publishing Co., 1977.

Katz, William. *Your Library—A Reference Guide*. New York: Holt, Rinehart and Winston, 1979.
(Describes the references found in the library and basic reference skills.)

Warren, Roland L. *Studying Your Community*. New York: The Free Press, 1965.
(A manual that covers many aspects of the community: health, education, recreation, housing, history, and problems. Includes survey methods and possible sources of community information.)

Wetherby, Terry, ed. *Conversations: Working Women Talk About Doing a Man's Job*. Millbrae, CA: Les Femmes, 1977.
(Interview with women in nontraditional jobs from butchers to bank presidents. Shows how questions, comments, and good listening skills can result in interesting and informative interviews.

Wigginton, Eliot, ed., *The Foxfire Books*. Garden City, NJ: Anchor Press, 1980.
(This is a good example of what can happen when students and teachers go into the community to research

topics. The result is a series of books based on interviews with craftspeople, artisans, and persons with special knowledge and skills. Topics cover a wide range of interests, from crafts and ghost stories to log cabin building, herbal lore, and other "affairs of plain living.")

Wurman, Richard, ed. *Yellow Pages of Learning Resources*. Cambridge, MA: Massachusetts Institute of Technology Press, 1972.

Index